The River of Life

by Robert Hale

Published by
YABISA GASHOUSE
C/ R. Curtoys Gotarredona, 1, Esc. 2, 2B
07840 Santa Eulària des Riu
Spain

Cover images: Details of stained glass at Nelson Cathedral,
New Zealand. "The River of Life", (Te Waioranga) designed
and created by Nelson glass craftsman, Len White. Public
domain.

ISBN: 978-84-949638-3-4

Find Robert Hale's poetry at:
www.roberthalepoetry.wordpress.com
www.nobettertimethanthis.tumblr.com
www.instagram.com/roberthale.poetry

And he showed me a river of water of life, bright as crystal,
proceeding out of the throne of God and of the Lamb.

Revelation 22:1

The happiness of the drop is to die in the river.

Abu Hamid al-Ghazali

ROBERT HALE

Foreword

This is my third collection of poems[1]. These poems were written over the course of the last fifteen months, inspired by the beauty of nature, the human condition, the mystery of the world, and of course, love. And this time, something else… the death of both my parents, within twenty days each other, in January 2019. This collection is especially dedicated to them.

Santa Eulària des Riu, Eivissa[2], 28/12/18.

---

1   My first poetry book was *No Better Time than This,* independently published on CreateSpace Independent Publishing Platform, 2018, republished by Yabisa gashouse, 2019. *The Storyteller of Isfahan* was pubished by Yabisa Gashouse in 2019.

2   Eivissa is the local name for Ibiza, where a dialect of Catalan is spoken.

Contents

ROBERT HALE

Dedication

To my parents, who taught me a sense of wonder
and a love of words. They passed from the river
to the ocean in January 2019.

To Ralph Lee Cuthbertson, who at ten minutes
past two on the morning of 17th November 2019
was thrust into the main stream, a few hours
after the publication of this book was
announced, thus making Bob, my fellow fisher
of the River of Life, a grandad.

October is the most beautiful month to be in Ibiza…

October Beautiful

October beautiful
Pearled horizon, orange pink
And turquoise falling soft
Away to golden high
On deep and gently puckered glass
The bumbling bee
Sweet of heath and thyme
The flitting bird
Through trembling vine
Gifts the world her morning song
Nameless, she needs not fame
Nor anything but her song
Which sings, there is nothing
But this day
Along this forest way
This brightly, freshly morn
This autumn dawn
This October beautiful

Santa Eulària des Riu, Eivissa, October 2018.

I'm sure we have all thought about what happens afterwards at some time or another…

Conversation with a Wise Woman About Reincarnation

I'm banking on reincarnation
Step down at a different station
Pour myself one more glass of wine
A little further down the line
Said I.

And She asked why, and I:
You see, the story isn't finished yet
There's still a vital tension there
Here I write, to lay it bare
This tiny coalescence of awareness
Will reach out to the void
Only a light year or so
Before it draws back into mortal form
To see again, through dusk, the dawn.

That's good, said she
And you? asked I
Not I, was her reply
And why, my love, my sweetest dove?
Because, she said, I'm happy with things
Just as they are
Happy just to fly afar.

Santa Eulària des Riu, Eivissa, October 2018.

When I was very small I was troubled by repetitive dreams with…

Visions of Awful Magnitude

A six-year-old child in dreams
Confronted by immensity
Impressions of infinity
Vistas of eternity
A world laid bare - a world, I say
Not just a globe, not just a planet -
In visions of awful magnitude
A monstrous hand grasps the stomach
Empty explodes jagged through the chest
Overwhelmed, the will, subdued
Withdraws into solitude
Confronted by immensity
The six-year-old was me

Again, again, a scene unfolds
Layer upon layers untold
Of hills in sweeping green, among them all
Villages uncountable, and then
The ocean stretching on and on
Of depths incomprehensible, above
The sky deepens into dark
Of voids inconceivable, in which
Perspectives beyond any count
Swallowed into nothingness
As by a dreadful sucking mouth

Again, again a scene unfolds

A scene of minutiae untold
Of detail so fine, so intricate
The human mind could never know
And within each single line or form
A whole new world is born
You feel the pull of every mark
Of every line and curve
You want to examine all you see
To look, to dwell, to delve
Yet terror stops you at the edge
For fear to lose the self

Again again the thought it strikes
The endlessness of things
A trillion paths and more from here
A minute decision made, a tiny action done
At any moment makes the way
And all happening at once
The thought it raves, it raves in vain
Too much to comprehend
For a six-year-old beneath the sheets
Awakened from his dreams

There, in that immensity
The child was as an ant, or less
Yes, infinitely less!
Such awesome insignificance
The child was less and less and less
The child was nearly nothingness
It pulled him, like a void
And there, deep in infinity
He felt the nothing sucking him

To shrink and disappear

The awfully large, the awfully small
The mysteries of time and space
The mysteries of infinity
Physicists have studied them all
Given them names and formulae
Made models to frame, to tame the world
In terms they think they comprehend
And through them all and at the end
With filters, with square-built frames
With tinted lenses, firm safeguards
We make it doable in our time, so long
As to withstand the unknown stream in spate
Our bridge is built in stone so strong

And so with grown-up, built-up buttressing
The world was made a doable thing
But if he sinks back down and in
Through swirls of mist he sees again
Those images of infinity
Feels their ceaseless silent wind -
The six-year-old in me

Santa Eulària des Riu, Eivissa, October 2018.

I am fascinated by dreams. They have in common with some poetry the abundant use of symbolism, and that is why some poetry has a dream-like quality. I think I know what prompted this dream. I had been revising a poem of mine called "The Word", in which one of the various ideas is that words today are often used carelessly, without thought or sensitivity. They have been diminished. And lo... That night I had a dream about a bookshop without books (words), whose owner is a charlatan, and which turns into a brothel (women used carelessly, without thought or sensitivity). What amuses me about this dream is the wit of the Madam. "May I interest you?", she asks. "Fuck you!", I reply. "That is just the point", she fires back. In a dream!

The Bookshop

I went into a bookshop, just to see what they
    had there
In the long white room all the walls were bare
A desk stood in the corner, bare save an empty
    vase
The charlatan Italian chief stared as I walked
    past
I climbed the winding staircase up to the
    second floor
A row of sturdy cubicles with wooden
    panelled doors
I'm in the wrong place, I think, I'd better go
    and soon
I took the other stairs and looked about as I
    went down
At the bottom of the stair, a freak came to my
    side
I'd seen his face before, he spoke - his tone
    was snide

Well, he said, is this the kind of place for you
    to go?
Defensively I said I'd learned it two moments
    ago
The extravagant fat lady, she's sitting by the
    door
As I approach she rises, asks may I interest
    you at all
I was getting flustered, said Fuck you, and
    your joint!
But she replied, my boy, the first is just the
    point
The freak is following my steps, a taunt upon
    his lips
I grab his tie and pull it hard, I'm fed up with
    his tricks

Ow, ow, hey, stop now! cries my lover in great
      alarm
I waken with a start, and see, I'm wrenching at
      her thumb
I'm troubled sometimes when I see such
      violence clouds my soul
But then life is for learning, or so I have been
      told

Santa Eulària des Riu, Eivissa, October 2018.[3]

---

3   Artwork: *The Fat Women* by Igor Grabar (1904), from Wikimedia Commons. Public domain.

To me the salmon is the ultimate representation of the power of the primary urge of all life: to reproduce...

The Mould of Salar

Brethren, sistren, we know three lives
Our first a sprig descending helter-skelter
Pushed by the stream, pulled by the unknown
Wanting nothing, knowing no end

Our second bound to deep black oceanic flows
Hunting with our brethren, sistren
Sleek fat feeding
Forgetting other, yet remembering too
Undefined yearnings growing
Plucking at our flesh
At last, to pull us bodily on
Wanting, running, knowing no end

Our third thrashing upwards through churning
    currents
Into worlds ever smaller, lighter, sweeter
Driven by an only end

An end which is two
To fill the Mould of Salar
While making way

Santa Eulària des Riu, Eivissa, November 2018.

This poem is an attempt to evoke the kind of animal fear felt during a nightmare...

The Horror in the Cavern

I will take you down there to show you
But we must take care
See how deep is this cavern
See how it gets dark up at the end
And yet there is a narrow sheaf of sickly light
I dare not go further there
But look you, up by this rock wall
A sort of shelf, and above
Strange signs, etched therein
But we must not linger long
I feel it, the presence is there
Back behind the end
Evil, predatory, nameless
Hateful, unholy intelligence
A disgusting horror
A terror to the soul
Immeasurably worse than pain, mutilation, death
Or any cruelty that humans can do
We must leave now
It is there, there
With that sickly light behind the dark
Make haste and leave this place!

Santa Eulària des Riu, Eivissa, November 2018.[4]

____

4   First published in Jitter, Issue #8, Prolific Press, 2019.

Real things are simply intricate rather than simplistically complicated. But people will more readily invest their belief in the latter kinds of things, to the point of their dogmatic defence, if they present an enigmatic facade and the promise of "amazing" (and easily gained) solutions...

The Collector of Bugs

O man, O woman,

Who cleverly take essence and pollute it with
  complication

Who observe not a thing of simple intricacy
  but to meddle

Painting upon it prettily with elaborate and
  fantastic forms

Symbols of beliefs cheaply bought but worn
  hard

Like exotic hats carried loud upon the head

The creeping fibres of their cloth growing in

Or emblems emblazoned richly down white
  robes

So captivating you will never take them off

Who, treating inclinations as knowledge, say
  often, "It is so"

Ever afraid of saying, "How can I know?"

Who, delivering clever discourse dressed as
  wisdom

Ever afraid to say, "I stand naked"

Whose artefacts bind you to the ground where
  you stand

With whose net of knots you yourself enmesh

With whose barbed hooks you yourself
  ensnare

And the more the hooks upon your line

The more you flap on your deck like a boated
     fish

Your fixations are like the bookish
     entomologist's pins

Holding his beetles to their mounts

Behold!

How interesting they are to the collector of
     bugs!

And yet

How free of life

Santa Eulària des Riu, Eivissa, November 2018.[5]

____

5   Photo by Joe Mabel, part of Don Ehlen's Insect Safari collection on display at the Hiawatha Artists Lofts, Seattle, Washington, during a "Bugs and Beer" night. From Wikimedia Commons. Creative Commons licence CC BY-SA 3.0 (https://creativecommons.org/licenses/by-sa/3.0/legalcode).

Messages are all and everywhere for those who are receptive. Or are they?

Message Bearers

You hear a word, observe a happening
Say there! As though it were a sign or
      message sent
Just right in time and place for you!
Wise one, how right you were to say 'as
      though':
Message bearers are all and everywhere
For receptive passers through
To fill therein with meaning
Just right for them in time and place
As men and women do

Santa Eulària des Riu, Eivissa, November 2018.

How is it that we sometimes form immediate and lasting emotional attachments to places on very first acquaintance…?

Unremembered Memories

Those feelings of affinity
Acutely, inexplicably
Felt for places first seen
But never known before
Except, perhaps, in the pages of a book
That linger long
Like unremembered memories

Santa Eulària des Riu, Eivissa, November 2018.

A metaphysical rumination...

The Lane We Walk Along

I can see just halfway down the lane we walk
along
There the curling mist obscures the further
view
I think it must be just as beautiful beyond
As it is behind
The going here is good, the map is true
But who will know this way once the map is
lost?
Or when the lane itself is naught but gravel
under forest roots?

We hear a cello playing through an open
window as we pass
The gaslight seems to flicker with its pitch and
strength
The notes sound well but fade as distance
reaches back
Of a beauty strangely heightened from afar
Their loveliness follows close upon our steps
Will any remain that tells, through the heavy
silence of the mist?
Who moves to the tune when the cellist lays
down her bow?
I read from a book I found along the way
A poem at once bewitching and bewitched
That pulsed and breathed and took to wing
Then as I read, flew and danced as real before
my eyes

But my eyes grew dim before I reached the
        end
Leaving sorest longing in my heart
The book abandoned now is turned to dust
That rises from the tread of travellers next
How long can what flew forth bewitch?
Or has bewitching vanished with the book?

A photo flutters in the breeze, jumping on, one
        step away
I see your smile again as it takes to air, too
        quick to catch
A smile in your eyes to pump the heart and
        burst
Will the smile remain when the photo pulps to
        mud in rain?
Or parches yellow and cracks under the
        harshly biting sun?

My love, my friend, my father, mother,
        brother, cousin all
My fellow seekers met, my fellow walkers
        arm-in-arm
Who with us have shared a way upon the lane
Through curling mist the cellist notes we
        loved
The poet's words like siren song upon our ears
Your countenance we loved as one of us and
        more
Your footfall of our life as much as of your
        own
Will we hear it once our flesh is washed to
        earth?
Will your time with us have sense once our

bones and yours
Are dust on the lane, or gravel under forest
    roots?

Purposes and purpose, awareness and
    awarenesses
Meanings, meaning, feelings, feeling
Connections and connection
All of this and nothing
In a flickered gaslight flame, refracted
Through a cellist's window pane
On the lane we walk along
Before the curling mist
Obscures the view

Yorkshire, England, November 2018.[6] [7]

---

6   First published in Poetry Quarterly, Fall 2018, Prolific Press, 2019.
7   Photo by Regenia Fondren, via Pixy.org, Creative Commons licence CC0 1.0 (https://creativecommons.org/publicdomain/ zero/1.0/legalcode).

This poem was inspired by the legend of Zlatorog, a magical gold-horned chamoix which once inhabited the mountain of Triglav ("Three Heads" or "Three Peaks") in Slovenia. The Triglav Rose (*Potentilla nitida*) is said to have grown from the spilled blood of Zlatarog...

Wash Down to Me Your rose in Blood

Oh, wash down to me your rose in blood
Three-headed one
Wash down to me my hunter love
For what use have I for your rose?

Oh, why did you come to me at all
Golden-headed boy
Who left for me your snow-skinned mothers
Among your flowered slopes?

Oh, but I am a jackdaw, curses upon me!
Brave hunter boy
I mocked you for the merchant's gold
With a hero's task that never could be won

Oh, from your garden in the clouds do bring
Love-struck one
The mad goat's golden horn, or else
A magic rose in winter bloom

Oh, would that you were ugly, dull and grey
O Golden Horn
Standing high in glinting morn
Shining to the hunter's bow

Oh, you flew so fast, so straight and true
Sharp-pointed one
The goat's blood from its flank did spill
Burning hot through snow

Oh, from red drops on snow you grew
Pink-headed one
A life from death in every pretty bloom
Each petal salve for the arrow's wound

Oh, how you charged so swift and strong
Immortal dazzle-horn
My hunter blinded, hunted now
The cliff too near, the arrows gone

Oh, wash down my fool, my hero in the melt
Clear-watered one

A clutch of flowers pink in winter bloom
His proof of love in vain

Oh, where have you taken your ladies fair?
Bearded spirit one
Oh, what of the treasure you laid to waste?
Neither to be seen again.

Oh, wash down to me your rose in blood
Three-headed one
Wash down to me my love
For what use have I for your rose?

Santa Eulària des Riu, Eivissa, December 2018.[8]

---

8   Photo by Michael R. Perry, *ZLATOROG*, *The Golden Horned Chamois Buck of Mt. Triglav*, via Flickr.com, reproduced according to Creative Commons licence CC BY 2.0 https://creativecommons.org/licenses/by/2.0/legalcode).

From the waters we came and to the waters we shall return...

A Sign from Home

I remember all those years back
For an instant in your giant creature's eye
I saw that it knew
Now I have gazed over you, upon you, for
     forty years and more
Studied your surface east and west, south and
     north
Plumbed your depths with eye of mind
Always alert for a sign
It has not come... but will

You live in many faces
Forty thousand tints and shades and hues
Today heavy, colour of lead
You speak with many voices
A million plays of pitch and tone
Of rhythm and strength
Today the slow, low moan
I wait for a sign in your face, your voice
I am sure, when I know it
Your creature, surfacing, will see it in my eye
In recognition we will join

We are close, you and I, and your creature
Like it, from you I came and to you I will
     come again
Your waters fill my veins, like its own

Impersonal, but to me
You feel like a most beloved friend, like home
And when the time comes for you to act
When you call your waters back
Come to you I must
I will have no other choice
But to trust

Santa Eulària des Riu, Eivissa, December 2018.[9]

---

9   Photo by Three-shots, via Pixabay.com, reproduced according to the
     Pixabay licence (https://pixabay.com/service/terms/#license).

Scenes from a repetitive dream...

Unreachable

Images that come and come again
Like ghosts
Never can they be held

A path weaves bleak across a shallow grassy
    rise
Large boulders here and there about the land
Then, a saddle wide across to the greater
    climb
There the way goes up and round the
    mountain's pleated skirts
On an outer bend a way station, a little
    teashop stop
Though high, we are but on the lower slopes
And up the trail, that unremembered
    wilderness
I want so much once more to travel on
To where I have travelled before
But always time runs out, the image fades
Before I make the way

I know the river bend lies beyond the wood
    and over the hill
Descend the cliff and there, a spot of rarest
    beauty
Wide and deep the river goes with rocky
    islands off the bend
And then, downstream the shallows ripple in
    delight

Warm is the sun in late afternoon
Oh, to dive and swim under waters clear and
    sweet
To breathe like the trout, hunt and play like
    the otter
But always darkness falls, the air comes cold
Before I make the river bank

By the sea there's a beach that stretches away
    beyond sight or thought
A place I know so well and yet again know
    not at all
The way there etched rough and deep into my
    bone
So many times I've joined the waves in play
Each time I sorely yearn to play again
But summer dwindles to chill and dark
And as I run the sun's last rays are fading fast
And as I go I lose the way I know so well
And always winter's curtain falls
Before I make the shore

Images that come and come again
Like phantoms
Never to be held

Santa Eulària des Riu, Eivissa, December 2018.[10]

---

10 First published in Poetry Quarterly, Summer 2019, Prolific Press, 2019.

A whole life may turn upon a small thing, a chance encounter, an apparently banal decision...

the organ grinder

an organ grinder standing in the square, he's **lame,** turns the handle, the tune always the **same,** he **squints,** in his eye the sinking winter solstice sun, it **glints,** catches yours as you walk **past,** pierces like a shard of **glass,** you **shiver,** and with its cup of **silver** the monkey from his shoulder **jumps,** towards you **runs,** you start, walk away in haste, the cup left empty in its **paws,** but the tune today was only **yours**

the organ grinder's **splinter** works in deep and **deeper,** cocoons under your **skin,** still the raw air cuts your **bone,** you know you'd had a **coin,** or two, you wish you'd **dared,** you wish you'd **spared** them to the monkey running to you in **vain,** across the **square,** but it's **OK,** next **day** you'll go to him once **more,** but the unchanged tune is **yours,** making all regrets in **vain,** the organ grinder's **gone,** the square left **bare,** the very town seems now a vacant **place,** next week the **same,** and then the same **again,** never more will he **come,** but the glint of his squint eye **remains,** will never leave but haunt your **days,** you **may,** you guess, see it **gleam** upon your dying **breath**

naked you lie **awake, thinking... sinking** in
the hot and heavy **night**, twenty years and
more have **passed**, out the open window
glancing **stars**, through half-closed lashes
pierce like **shards**, pierce your languor,
inwardly you **start**, they carry to you again
the **thought**, what would life have **brought**,
had not you passed that **way** that **day**... or
else, had made to **linger**, by the magic organ
grinder

Santa Eulària des Riu, Eivissa, December 2018.[11]

---

11 Photo from 1896, W. C. Brown Collection of the Ohio County Public
Library Archives, via Flickr.com. Public domain.

Sometimes, as I walk around the coastline of my island home, I write things on rocks. I call it ephemeral poetry, which of course it isn't as soon as I write it in a book like this. Never mind...

Now I Have Words

Now I have words
I remain unmoved
And yet
Do you see how our journey has changed?

Cala d'en Sardina, Eivissa, December 2018.[12]

---

12 Photo by the author.

Places, dreams and impressions all mixed up on an ordinary day...

Being in Many Places at Once

Up here on a day like this it feels a little
    like Dharamshala

A place to think of death and speak of other
    worlds

Rain trickles through the roof as you try to
    find your voice

Back in town a chill wind blows across you
    down the avenue

Purposeful clouds march steadily through

Of a sudden, a springtime day turns dark again
    to winter

You lift your face to the breeze, breathe deep

Fresh fills your nasal passages, into your
    cranial vault

Because at this moment you are; at the centre
    of all your pasts and futures

Along the streets and alleyways, walking
    beside walls, down steps

Through large squares, all of this unknown but
    known

Unable to make your way back to the
    completely familiar

And you look on but are not interested in all
    the ritual ceremony

And you have no patience with the ornate
    edifices, no matter how stylish

And sometimes you wish things had meaning,
    or else none at all

The empty little restaurant is filling with
        people you resent having to speak to
The pedant sits and asks for a morsel,
        complains of having to leave
        baksheesh
Words and conversations, words and
        conversations, words and
        conversations
And the philosopher tells his only story
        endlessly to the stars
You are attracted to the idea, you say, it's just
        it's told as truth
Instead of myth or fairy tale, but what then, is
        the difference?
Words and conversations, words and
        conversations, words and
        conversations
Like a flock of gulls around a trawler
Sometimes you wish things had truth, or else
        none at all

Outside the big round pine squeals with the
        mixed chatter of a thousand tiny birds
And the tall eucalyptus stands black against a
        yellowing sky
And the freak passing by tells of love and
        light, but the dark looks just as fine to
        you
And though you travel joyous in darkness'
        embrace, you keep your sabre handy
Against forces, that, impersonal and without
        blame though they may be
Make momentum of their own, incompatible
        and immune to those things

Down by the creek the leopard cubs peering
    from the canes
The shoals of young bass gliding in glinting
    brackish shallows
Make you realise here is this world and here is
    this life
So you walk carefully on
At the centre of all your pasts and futures
Because at this moment you are

Santa Eulària des Riu, Eivissa, January 2019.[13]

---

13 Photo by epidemiks, *Rainbow over McLeod Ganj, Himachal Pradesh*, via
Wikimedia Commons, reproduced according to Creative Commons licence
CC BY 2.0 (https://creativecommons.org/licenses/by/2.0/legalcode).

I wrote a poem about Ibiza called *Island*, which appeared in my second volume of poems[14]. It comprised the first and third of the following stanzas. It was twee and it didn't tell the whole truth. So I added stanzas two and four below…

Paradise Island

Little white house among dark hills
Patchwork squares the farmer tills
Pine trees blanketing slope and fold
Whitewashed church on rocky knoll

Smart villas stride across the slopes
With garden art for fashionable folks
Black stripes gouged on green and gold
Where lines of cockroach carriages crawl

Fishing boats rock in the dancing light
Boat houses sit round a tear-drop bight
Cliffs climb high from the rocks and scree
Swifts soar fast high above the sea

Beach clubs scramble to fence the shore
Polythene clothes the ocean floor
Chill-out blasts over waters wide
Power boats boom on the sickening tide

Santa Eulària des Riu, Eivissa, July 2018, January
2019.

---

14 *The Storyteller of Isfahan*, published by Yabisa Gashouse, 2018.

Some things, beyond words, we can listen to endlessly and still they bring joy...

Listening Still

Towers of rock stand wide at lips of bay
Cliff falls to boulders a mile below
Endless wash of sea of wave
Strong on land the chill will blow
Up and hissing trees a-high on ridge
Peaks around gold in early sun
Here below in shadow colours dark
Land birds flit through juniper and pine
Sea birds seaward gently cry
The rock on which I sit is damp and cold
A boat a-chugging slides across the bay
Endless wash of sea on rocks below
Is there anything that has not been said
      before?
And yet
I am listening still to ocean waves

Es Corrals, Santa Agnès, Eivissa, January 2019.

More rock poetry…

The Road Is Long

The road is long, rough, tortuous
But its end inevitable
In this we are equal

Es Corrals, Santa Agnès, Eivissa, January 2019.[15]

---

15 Photo by the author.

You never finished those things you were doing and never will. It
all just stopped there...

The Tools Are Down /
Unfinished Tapestry

The tools are down
The workshop empty
The hand that worked is still
The strings on the lute are broken
The writing book put back inside the drawer
The funny hat you wore stands dusty on the
      sill
The setting sun will squint your eyes no more

The studio is quiet
The skylight window closed
Drawings filed away, paints laid out in rows
The tapestry put down, a thread hangs loose
      and bare
The needle stuck for safekeeping in the
      cushion of the chair
Outside the flowers we planted all are
      withered or gone
The quarrelsome tangling weeds will suffer
      your trowel no more

Santa Eulària des Riu, Eivissa, February 2019.

It's the unique and unrepeatable locus in time and place, with all its specific associated sensory cues, that makes it feel just like...

A Time for Dying

You know
It is a time for dying
By the black lichen climbing up the grey stone
　　　walls
The brown moorland half-clothed in snow
The dark clouds that hang low and move slow
The lone kestrel watching from its post
The jet river that swishes the reeds so
　　　ceaselessly
And dusk creeps up so soon after dawn

The land is whist and frore
Some will never make it through
Now, life was short
And death is cold
The kestrel's eye is sharp
Impersonal

You dig your hand to earth
Scratch its scraping grit with broken nails
Raise your eyes, now the kestrel flutters high
You thrust your hand to river's flow
Feel it cut like sharpened steel
Hard and cold, and definite
The kestrel dives
You know

It is a time for dying

Yorkshire, England and Santa Eulària des Rio,
Eivissa, February 2018.[16]

<hr>

16 Photo by Chris Heaton, *Winter on Hanlith Moor*, via Geograph.org.uk,
reproduced according to Creative Commons licence CC-BY-SA 2.0 (https://
creativecommons.org/licenses/by-sa/2.0/legalcode).

It's a lovely feeling to be in love…

Today at the Railings by the Sea

Today I stopped at the railings by the sea
A cormorant stood on a rock
Just as it did
Those many years ago
And the silvery fish played in the pools
Just as they did
Those many years ago
And the glinting ripples washed your rock
Just as they did
Those many years ago
And a breeze touched my cheek like your
    touch
Just as it did
Those many years ago
When both of us wondered
What would happen next
And both of us wondered
What would become of it all
Those many years ago
When you sat on your ledge
On your early morning walk
And I came to the railings by the sea
Climbed down to sit with you
And you took my hand in yours
And said
It's a lovely feeling to be in love
Those many years ago.

Santa Eulària de Riu, Eivissa, February 2019.[17]

The next five poems were written during a trip to Malaysia in March/April 2019.

Toady in the Kitchen

Toady in the kitchen looking for flies
Pokes out his tongue then blinks his eyes
Toady in the kitchen old and wise
Sees no truths and tells no lies

Monkey in the tree tops sitting on a bough
Goes chirp-chirrup and fools around
Swings up high and swings low down
Throws a bitter apple to the ground

Gecko on the ceiling looking for flies
Pale as the moon in her disguise
Beats her tail and swallows her prize
Cik-cak cik-cak cick-cak she cries

Cicada in a rubber tree looking for a bride
Plays his tymbal, screeches loud
Lady's shy so she flies inside
But Toady's in the kitchen with his mouth
open wide

Froggy in the reeds at the edge of the pool
Watches the fun and laughs, hoo hoo

Stands up, falls down, fa fa foo foo
Froggy in the mud-pond laughing at you

"The Dusun", Pantai, Seremban, Negeri Sembilan,
Malaysia, March 2019.[18]

____

18 Photo by the author.

Jungle music…

The Doo Doo Doo Doo Bird

The Doo Doo Doo Doo Bird goes
Doo doo doo doo
And Gecko on the ceiling goes
Chik chik chik chik chik
The Waah Waah Bird goes
Waah waah waah waah waah waah waah
And the Dip Dap bird goes
Dip dap dop
The Haw Haw Bird goes
Haw haw haw haw haw
And the Hiccupy bird goes
Ber-loop
Cicada in the tree goes
Wee wee wee wee weeeeeeeeeee
And the silly old frogs all in time
Go ha ha hee ha ha hee hee

Doo doo doo doo
Chik chik chik chik chik
Waah waah waah waah waah waah waah
Dip dap dop
Doo doo doo doo
Haw haw haw haw haw
Wee wee wee wee weeeeeeeeeee
Ber-loop
Doo doo doo doo
Ha ha ha hee ha ha hee hee

Berembun Forest Reserve, Negeri Sembilan, Malaysia, March 2019.[19]

An ode to a city that over the past several years I have sort of fallen in love with. For its friendly people, its innate multiculturalism, its seductive blend of old and new, its green spaces, its quintessential Asia-ness, and above all for its sheer vibrancy. Kuala Lumpur was founded at the confluence of the rivers Gombak and Klang, and its name in Malay means, literally, "muddy confluence". The resulting river Klang, taking its name from the larger of the two tributaries, has recently been rebranded by the city authorities the "River of Life". The waterfront has been given a very superficial face lift, but the character of the river still remains… a drain!

River of Life

Where two waters meet
The Gombak and the Klang
Begins the drain
They've called the River of Life

Drain-river brown of mud and filth
Comfortably one with city air
Essence not bound by concrete banks
And the forest earth that runs her channels
Flows also through nasal passages
Into brains and into blood and lymph

Out on the forest, thunder growls
Its breath softly on the city
Scents of ancient mud
Exotic, potent, impregnate
With spice, scents of river
Brown of mud and filth
And its down-pouring refills the drain

Where waters meet begins the drain
They've called the River of Life
But that, is in the street
Where all creation creates
Vibrant in all its messy, miraculous form
And the smell of its decay
Rises strong as life from the drains
That fill the River of Life

And amazingly there
In that river of living decay
Brown of mud and filth
Rolling black backs and turning silver sides
Prove its potency manifest
To create again from decay
And in the street people from three directions

 meet
Do what they must, observe the rule, live the
 life
Create and recreate

And the quiet Malay gardener comes each day
 from the kampong
And the joyful Indian taxi driver has
 threadbare collar and cuffs
And the serious Chinese pharmacist looks
 over his glasses
Pores over his potions
And the rich families take lunch at the old
 club house
Where the waiters are white-coated, black tied
And the poor man on the corner strokes his
 one-stringed violin
And the poor lady on the pavement
 embroiders squares of cotton
And the beggars find better ways to beg
And the stunted invalid child sings for her
 supper
Down the bright-lit street where eight
 directions meet
And all around people eat and make for others
 to eat
And at the night stalls the sellers call out
Come come, young lady, nice bag, perfume
 Sir, a watch, Rolex
And by Central Market the conductor calls
Klang Klang Klang Klang Klang Klang Klang
And all the people hurry to board
The bus that goes to Klang

And at Jamek mosque men sleep in the shade
And under the dragon the people light incense
Gaining merit to smooth the way
Along the river of life
And the Tamils by the temple string their
    garlands
And inside, the unsmiling priest swaps
    blessings for bananas
And afterwards
Sits in the alcove, checks Youtube
In the city where every face has a smile
Except the very miserable
And the addicts, lying vacant by the drain
Their energies nearly done
Obeying the phase of decay
And their bodies know
For they gather at the meeting of the waters
Brown of mud and filth
Where begins
The River of Life

Kuala Lumpur, Malaysia, 24 March and 5 April
2019.[20]

---

20 Photo by the author.

It's a major tragedy. These breathtakingly beautiful wonders of the world, the coral reefs, are dying fast...

The Reef

From the sand Stingray knifes away
Surprising Slug, Urchin football-size
Turtle imperturbable, paddles by

A colourful rabble carries on its day
At the reef, all's a-bicker and a-squabble
Like the quarrelsome neighbours they are

Big Puffer puffs up and glides
Into a coral cave to hide
He's spotted black on white, big eyes

Clown struts out from Anemone, acting brave
Then darts back in at the prudent time
Noisy Parrot Fish chunters, chirps

Grumbling about the local quirks
Like a well-healed burgher in the square
And the ocean's far away

But beyond the boiling reef, unseen
A greyed-out graveyard closing in
It's almost time, my beauties, and the witness,
    I
Am a finger's hair on the hand of night

Tioman Island, Malaysia, April 2019 and Santa
Eulària des Riu, Eivissa, May 2019.[21]

Death comes as a shadow...

Fish Trap

Flesh glazed in a thousand blazing hues
A multiform clutch of breathing brilliances
Shifting, listless, with unquiet calm
No more do they urge to explore
They have spent their choices in this new
      world
Thus, they are still, or drift
Bewildered in their ignorance
Of a new situation
But agitate and move away
As I, the alien, approach

Flat eyes stare but what is seen?

The new world is strongly framed
But of unknown stuff
The breathing things know the now but not the
      path by which the now arrived
They see the there but not the way by which
      the there connects with them
Or could be reached
They know the now but cannot see the after-
      now

Fabulous coated breathing things
Your fate is read
You know it not
But feel fear

As a dark form looms above

Tioman Island, Malaysia, April 2019, and Santa
Eulària des Riu, May 2019.[22]

---

22 Photo by Matt Kieffer, *Fishing trap / pot*, via Flickr.com, reproduced
according to Creative Commons licence CC BY-SA 2.0 (https://
creativecommons.org/licenses/by-sa/2.0/).

A dream of bereavement. Suddenly the ground on which you stand
seems not so stable. Life is...

Precarious

Then, you were there, across the breach
I went to you where you stood; we walked
I'm glad I could see you before you left, you
    said
And I, you're looking so well, so good

Then father from the other side
Called, now bring her to me here
And the tunnel went from left to right
As it always does. The sight

Though once forbidding, was not that day
And through we went and you skipped down
While I took careful steps, afraid
To climb across the steep decline

Then of a sudden I must leave
A kiss, a hurried goodbye
But from the side I fell away
Far far down
Far down
Away

Santa Eulària des Riu, Eivissa, May 2019.

A single death happens at the end of an instant. While the play of life is all around. You are never separate from all of this.

Footsteps at dawn

Whose footsteps are those that crunch the
    gravel?
Are they mine, or are they of the world itself,
    or more?

Son, I see you with me now; look how the
    dawn is bleak
See the cloud settled upon John Andrew's
    Peak

A rabbit runs in the morning; whose pretty
    talons were those
That squeezed a brother in the night? The
    owl's, or yours
Or something other?

It is good to travel the moonless night, there's
    such beauty there
But in truth the daytime too is good; come,
    let's walk on through

Look you well, son, many things can trap the
    eyes
Step with sunlit joy, but care, ever mindful of
    the trail

The pigeon turns its head from death, half a

second too long

The end of an instant is enough, will it take to
    wing again?

This mosquito on my hand enjoys my blood
    too much

Now I am master of its fate; but feeding on
    whose blood am I?

On whose hand do I rest?

Son, are those your steps that tread so light
    and yet so sure?

Or are they of the world itself, or more?

Santa Agnès de Corona and Santa Eulària des Riu,
Eivissa, May 2019.[23]

---

23 Photo from Pxhere, reproduced according to Creative Commons licence
CC0 (https://creativecommons.org/publicdomain/zero/1.0/legalcode).

As we poison our environment, we poison ourselves. Is that much not clear, or is it just unimportant?

Reciprokarma / Egosystem

My lover, your vessels, lavish with rushing,
    pulsing blood
And gently seeping lymph, are but my own;
Those who corrupt them suck the poison with
    our blood
For we are the rolling rivers, the sparkling
    streams and all the dark waters

All my daughters, all my sons, their
    heartwood is my own sinew
Their rich earth is my flesh, which in their
    depth resides
Those who cut them tear asunder their very
    own limbs
Those who burn and scorch them breathe of
    our own wood smoke

My good friends, your Great Ocean with
    storm and calm and current
You are sea of mind; our shores are washed by
    ancient waters
I who foul them find my spirit as a shredded
    rag fouled high upon the rocks
One day, who knows? the waves might reach
    those shreds and draw them back

My fathers, my mothers, and all my people
I am the handkerchief that fell from your

> pocket
> Help me peg it to the line, together we'll
> watch it blow
> And breathe in deep the wind from North or
> West

Santa Eulària des Riu, Eivissa, May 2019.[24]

----

24 Photo by Maaark, via Pixabay.com, reproduced according to the Pixabay licence (https://pixabay.com/service/terms/#license).

I think I will leave this one an enigma...

Saint Joan Accidentally

For all of them you bled your heart and spilled
    your tears
Lepers, conjurers, angels; innocents, liars and
    thieves
Your crystal tears etched trails red-raw upon
    your flesh
Your heart-blood scorched your veins in holy
    flame
You haven't been a perfect saint, but then
    again you are more pure than that
Although you never realised the cost, and
    even now
While you pay, in endless pain
And burn upon the fire they built for Joan
You will deny it would have made a difference

Santa Eulària des Riu, Eivissa, May 2019.

The air of spring, perhaps, made me desire a return to simplicity…

Not Doing

Last night I tore up all my books
Watched the pieces flutter random to the
      ground
Was that wise?
The morning's zephyr has brushed my skin
I've heard the rushes whisper
And birds begun to sing

Santa Eulària des Riu, Eivissa, May 2019.[25]

---

25 Photo by the author.

The last time I saw my father...

Stone Cold

They say "stone cold" but stones can be warm
What about "death cold"?
Or "hands-scratching-gravelly-winter-earth
      cold"?
Or "Benfleet-Marsh-in-February-with-east-
      wind cold"?
It's not right anyway
That's not you
Not your nose, too pointed
Not your cheeks, too gaunt
Not your lips, too thin
Not your mouth, too wide
Not your smile at all
With those silly upturned bits at the ends
Instead of yours, full and hearty
I mean, you did, sometimes
Smile
And the dark blood collected at your finger
     tips
Where, I see, they should have cut your nails
And your skin is
Benfleet Marsh in February skin
But of course, I had forgotten
You've just come out
Of the fridge
And I'd never seen mother cry before

He always liked his hair stroked, she said
As she did it one more time

Santa Eulària des Riu, Eivissa, May 2019.[26]

------

26 Artwork: *Woman Mourning* by Vincent Van Gogh, from Wikimedia Commons. Public domain.

Remember, remember...

When the World Was New

Remember the smell of new-mown grass
In the morning glistened sweet with dew
And warmly bathed by the day's young sun
We could never walk but run
When the world was new
Remember we woke to the blackbird's song
And the hurry to be outdoors
Running in the endless field
Picking puffballs from the lawn
Or eating damsons from the tree
The days ahead stretched out so long
The ones behind so few
We felt contented, live and free
When the world was new

Remember going with Dad to town
On buses green and blue
And sat by the window looking through
At red and yellow cranes so high
(They climbed up nearly to the sky)
And all the people walking by
When the world was new
Remember when we were strangers here
When the world called out to us so bright
And down on the beach the waves of blue
Lapped forever at our feet
We hadn't forgotten what we knew

But stood arms stretched and tried to reach
The land across the great big sea
Back when the world was new

Santa Eulària des Riu, Eivissa, May 2019.[27]

---

27 Photo by tzviell, via Pixabay.com, reproduced according to the Pixabay
licence (https://pixabay.com/service/terms/#license).

Gargantuan faces smile complacently from posters. With stupid slogans. Local election time is here. I need to get away, in search of fresh air...

The Pedlars of Calle San Juan

On San Juan the pedlars polish their smiles
As I pass they shine them in my eyes
They intend to dazzle, it's an art
One is well to do, dressed smart
Dependable, capable
She's playing an easy part
Her eyes say, as she adjusts
Her perfect mask, she trusts
It's full well understood
She's just like my own flesh and blood

The other's coat is brown and rough
The wearer's face set firm but soft
Lines etched darkly in the flesh
Of quiet wisdom, constructed to express
Unbending determination, yet nevertheless
Tempered by compassion
(And without regard for fashion)
Honesty and clarity
Principles, integrity
And of course he's just like you and me
A fellow farer of the sea

These folk all have big faces
Larger than life, most literally

They flap a little in the breeze
Shine their twinkling eyes in mine
And one is selling my heart's desire
The other all that I deserve
Poured into goblets made of gold, but first
They want a glassful of my soul
But right at this moment herein
I am not for dealing

A fortune teller on the bridge
She wants her palm of silver
She takes my hand, her smile is sweet
Dig out a coin to give her
But answer me a question do
I have a difficult choice to make
Do I deserve my heart's desire?
Do I wish what I deserve?
Do the pedlars know, and who
Decides? I am confused I must aver
Do they know the answers?
Are those people in the posters
Real or just imposters?

She pointed down some steps of stone
She did not speak
But smiled again, and there I went, alone

At the creek, the air is fine and clear and crisp
The ducks all bicker over illicit little bits
Of bread, but all sit pretty in the pool
From a branch above my head a turtle dove
In the eucalyptus tree coo-roos

A shoal of small grey mullet goes
Slowly up the stream
Nosing the surface as it moves
A moorhen in the rushes clucks
Flashing her little red throat
A white Scottie dog lifts a leg, claims a
    jasmine bush
Whose sweet thanks calls the breeze

And somehow here, the air so crisp and clear
Has spoke; these water folk
Convince the more
They seem more true and real
Than the fancy pedlars in the street
Whose faces now are fading fast
Like the phantom wisps of smoke
They are

Santa Eulària des Riu, Eivissa, May 2019.

They say that to begin meditation one must focus on one thing. I focused on a palm frond waving in the breeze. But my meditation turned into an interesting perceptual experiment, and then a poem (so that's *nil points* for meditation)...

Frond

Morning May breeze of sea
This swaying to and fro
Joyfully familiar
A morning, how surprising!
How good!
This we have known before!

And there sits the man we have known
On the balcony over there, gazing over here
At who he is
I know he is the man I used to be
And the man he will become
But this, here...
He is now this one

Whose brothers brush his skin
Whose dryness rustles in our ears
Whose chlorophyll bends his temporal lobes
Infuses through his skin
See him, the gazing, swaying man!

Though you can tell, of late
His swaying
Has grown a little rusty

Santa Eulària des Riu, Eivissa, May 2019.[28]

—————————————
28 Photo by the author.

After shedding the skin of its immature form (the nymph), the adult mayfly lives out its life in a single day. Every second is precious...

Mayfly

Late May
A glory day
The swarming of the fly
Her rising-falling lovers' dance
Clouds the air from dusk to dark
Then, swooning on the river flat
She yields new life as she lays back
Her carpet on the water brown
Her energies full expended then
Her eggs sink to the river bed
A whole life lived just in a day
That is her way, ordained
And you, my friend
You have your chance
What will be your glory dance?

Santa Eulària des Riu, Eivissa, May 2019.

Even such a low-status, commonplace life form as the herring illustrates the wonder and the mystery of life. What's it all about?

The Significance of the Herring

What strange way is this in a world of
    strangeness?!
Off the coast a herring shoal a hundred million
    strong
So close packed and turning this way that way
    all as one
Vast and perfect living thing
Then five giants, humpbacks each of thirty ton
Rise they too, as one, and breaking surface
    yawn
Five dreadful giants' mouths… and there
Five thousand herring gone!
Funnelled flapping into five gaping giant
    throats

What mystery is this in a universe of
    mysteries?!
At an instance physics and chemistry combine
Behold! There and then life will become
To create its form and ever outward wind
Like creeping root-stalks breaking barren land
Then, sprouting upward hardy shoots of green
It twines pointless atoms fast into a vital sum

Sucked down the throat of gulping Whale
The wriggling herring sees its death but does
    not think

It feels the jolt of fear but does not dread

Feels the pain of crushing maw but does not
    suffer for its life

This herring shoal might as well be grass on
    rain-spilled veldt

Grazed by herds of roaming wildebeest

Tons of wriggling life becoming the others'
    feed... and yet

Just as grasslands give and give again

Herring spawn will turn these coastal waters
    white

For yards five thousand long, by one hundred
    wide

Thus life withdraws and comes again

Just like an ever-changing tide

And I am left open-mouthed, mouthing
    disarticulated thoughts

Wondering what…? Just what in the world is
      this
Endless eating of thing by bigger thing?
Is there a plan, what is the scheme?
Or shall I just affix my lengthening beard of
      grey, and say
There is no plan that you can understand
There is no scheme, it all… just is

Says to me the herring, I live to spawn to live
      again
Says to me the whale, the little fish exist for
      me to eat
For strength to mate and spawn and live again
Says the krill to me, this great herring is a
      worthy tyrant
To escape and spawn and live again
Says the Earth to me, it is a vital link
In the chain for things to spawn and live
And live and spawn and live again
But thinks to me the universe's epic noiseless
      expanse
And the word that comes to mind is "Mind"
Say I, my word! I have been blind!

Climbing up a patterned strand of ribboned
      plaits
Moving through layered sequences of
      predation
Further up and further on in Mind
At its perfect apex, there it shall prevail
It seems there is but one greater life
To live and spawn and live again

All for one for all to nourish Mind
That the zenith be approximated further day
        by day

Deep as the dark giants of the sea is Mind
Potent and wide-watching as all the hunters of
        the land
Bright and swift as all the coloured riders on
        the wind
Yet still juvenile,
Its mastery, while great, is incomplete
Its wisdom, while silent, has yet to speak
As with the flapping herring, the risks are
        great
It is not ready, so it must wait
Like the eaglet's dance, wobbly on an
        outspread branch
It opens its wings, intends, but does not
        chance
The inconceivable dive or jump or thrust
So wait it must

Spawn colours the coastal waters white
For yards five thousand long, one hundred
        wide
For what, in the end, this thing so strange?
One vital link, or many lives lived out in vain?
Will Mind shimmer, will it thrill, or in the end
Will it fail?
Will it make the purest thrust, its tender petals
Fanning out in gorgeous summer bloom?
Will the Eaglet's timid talons soar?
Will young Whale dive deepest as it must?

Or will Mind get trapped, growing thin and
    wan
Like autumn's waning moon, dipping slow
    behind a fog
Or, suffering a mighty shock,
Will it break apart, dissolve to almost
    nought... again...
The lowly to inherit Earth
For years ten million more
Of dearth
Another writing of the score
Another playbook to rehearse

Santa Eulària des Riu, Eivissa, June 2019.[29]

---

29 Photo by Axel Kuhlmann, *Herrings,* via PublicDomainPictures.com, reproduced according to Creative Commons licence CC0 1.0 (https://creativecommons.org/publicdomain/zero/1.0/ legalcode).

A story of unbelonging and longing, alienation and heartache, on the balcony across the alleyway...

The Crying Woman

I wonder what happened to the woman
who cried and smoked every day
on the balcony across the way
of the flat where she lived with her man
and the others who went and came
and sometimes a girlfriend would drop by
and they sat and drank a glass of wine
and they talked and smoked
and didn't cry but smiled
and laughed, and it broke
the silent days when she sat
alone and smoked
and put her face in her hands
and cried.
And she was quite pretty before, but then
grew drab and pale and gaunt.

Crying woman, every day,
on the balcony across the way.

I like to think she's gone
back to a place that feels like home
and there, among her own
she smiles and laughs
and is pretty again.
But maybe not, maybe now

in another town
on another balcony
across another way
of another unhappy foreign land
she smokes and cries every day
with her face hidden in her hands.

Crying woman, every day,
on the balcony across the way.

Santa Eulària des Riu, Eivissa, June 2019.[30]

30 Photo by Kat Jayne, via Pexels.com, reproduced according to the Pexels
licence (as 02/01/2020 viewable at https://www.pexels.com/photo-license/).

There is an old quarry by the sea called *Sa Pedrera*, rebranded "Atlantis" by the hippies and new agers. It is a place of magical beauty. But what then is magic?

Finding Magic at the Old Quarry

I walk down to the old quarry
Taking many paths and one
Trodden through stunted juniper and thorn
Here over rock, there on fine sand
The bay is still in shadow as I go down
The morning ripples cool the skin
To be abroad in the world on a day so fine!

A fishing boat slides across the bay over east
Cormorants scud away, low to the water
All is beautiful and strange
The shore a table of rock wide and flat
Little cairns and symbols carved
A rectangle room, open to the sky
Straight corners, steps, geometrically aligned
Scrawled patterns, graffiti
Profound, banal, poetic
A worn-out dragon. A phallus.
Poseidon's three-pronged spear
A monkey's face, a pregnant female body
People's names, initials with dates
Somebody carves in stone they are
The starlight of the other's path

This the nature of humanity
To cast a human face
On nature's incomprehensibility
Magic flames the spirit in man
To make believe and to believe
To become a Believer

O fabrications of the mind!
You are indeed infinite!
In number, in wisdom, also in worthlessness!
How you manipulate to gain your aims!
With scientific endeavours, magical
          formulations
In concrete reality and smoky mirage
For the further one reaches, inwards or out
The deeper, the wider one sees
The more the concrete crumbles
As the sandstone where I sit turns so easily
To the sand I leave behind me on the path

These marks in rock, these piles of stones
Embodiments of awe and struggle
To make of wonder and affinity felt
A scheme, a code, a sacred truth
To fix, to own, to share, belong
Take care! The etched mark has potency
Of binary valency
Catalyst of the infinite
Or a band of iron tightly locked around the
          skull
The key mislaid, lost in time
Therein lies the magic; this I will tell

But I, too, am The Believer
I believe in the process of nature
I believe in the power of the human mind
What could be more magical than these?
My spirit ignites in magic!

Santa Eulària des Riu, Eivissa, June 2019.[31]

---

31 Photo by the author.

Another dream. Dad always wished to analyse things, explain them. Mum was more tolerant of not knowing...

Flying Lessons

The wind blows clouds across the sky
Spray off dancing waves spits wild
The many-spangled hill is bare
And gently seated there
Mother tells her tale
The world comes dark, the world comes light
The April sun's at play
Among the bending flower heads, is Hare

Above him Hawk Wing flutters high
Her head cocks slightly to the side, her eye
Piercing her prey
Then father, watching, from his chair
Begins to tell of flight
The tail tilts thus, the wings must turn just so
    and so
But mother turns her head instead
With far-off gaze
To where the blue meets blue, and says
Th Pixabay ese things are very old, how strange
We think we know of what is told
Or what we tell
Now on the hill Hare has run
And Hawk Wing wheels away

Santa Eulària des Riu, Eivissa, June 2019.[32]

As I go through life I try to whittle things down. To achieve bare simplicity. As I go through life, too, I gradually cast off my certainties. The aim is to master navigation in uncertain waters...

The Bonesetter

Life is simple, time is long
Tonight I file a piece of bone
A bridge for father's mandolin
A monotonous task, but pleasant
Pointless, as I cannot well tune it
As I tune a person's body
But then
Pointlessness too may have its worth

File rubs on bone
Bone dust floats like smoke
A train moves across the plain
Slowly carrying the years
It whistles long each night
Telling the passing of each day
For that I have no fear

This bone is hard and brittle
It is good, solid, tastes of earth. I like
The fine powder falling from the file
Its burnt scent in my nose
So many years bones have been my work
Not like this, but living bone
That bends a little to the strain
Living bone and flesh and blood and lymph

And pain, and other kinds of hurt ...

And life itself

You know, for me the world is flat
A wheelwright made me four wheels
To make with them a cart
And in the cart I roll across the plain
Like that lonely evening train
Where I go, I gather weeds
Or so they are called by some
Weeds for food and weeds to heal

Once I travelled that iron road
To the edge of the ocean
Gazed to the far horizon
I saw a mast appear, get taller
Then the hull of a great ship
Seafarers sail from port in one direction
And come to the place left moons ago
They say that men in space
Would see the world as a ball
But I have no desire to travel so far

The doctor in the town will save a life
And willy-nilly cause another to end
In the one case he is clever
In the other the disease is bad
His time is short, but mine is long
I do not aspire to much
But I can bend a joint and give a herb
Tune the body and touch the mind

And see health flow and grow

This is enough for my flat world
But do not talk to me of cure
The only one I know is six feet down
Once I wished for certainty
A path alive with briars
Invisible at first, until you trip

I learned to walk uncertain lands
Tramping long upon that plain
The weather unstable but the heart is calm
Where rising dust dims the view
I sense the way the same
So far, so good
My life is simple, my time is long
I file my piece of bone

Santa Eulària des Riu, Eivissa, June 2019.

Ancient philosophers were acute observers of the natural environment. They intuited how life is conditioned by a few basic phenomena. Nature is so wonderfully basic ("elementary") that it induces such reflections...

Elemental

Vapour lifting after-storm
Between the warming peaks
While glinting waters tumble
Through bare rock of white
And slopes of gently sighing pine

It is the golden time of day
When sunlight hovers in shafts above the
      valley floor
Before the sun fuses to the ridge
And twilight folds the world
In time of shadow

A breeze, evening-strengthened, sweeps the
      vale
Fans this fire built on river stone
Whose flames rejoice, bound and spark
The dried cast-offs fed to them
From blessed children of the earth

The wind sings the trees
The water plays the stones
And tempered by the after-rain
The flames sink down again
To shyly dart through gaps

And lick around the curves

A hand stokes the fire
Heat-red, strong of winding vein
Lusty muscle, creased in palm
Scaffolded of knuckled bone
Ash and dirt on skin a-daub
And dug beneath the earth-rough nails

The land itself is in this hand
Fire and water, valley breeze
Rock and storm, rising steam
Green of tree, shafts of sun
And within this earth
My own blood and lymph do run

Rio Bianco, Friuli, Italy, July 2019.[33]

33 Photo by the author.

When one discovers that somehow one is now more distant, and more joyful...

Something Has Changed

At the bars and coffee shops
Sitting all the cittadini
Sipping all cappucci
Spritz or prossecchini

Thumbing through the Sports Gazette
Juve doing well, but not there yet
Talk of politics, immigration
Our nation, damnation
Just gets worse and worse
And men gesticulate and curse

Browsing all smart boutiques
Down the smart shopping street
Housewives well-to-do
Walk the walk every week
No surprises, nothing new
No change down the avenue

In the castle garden
Looking south into the haze
Then with deliberation
Turning north to face the hills
And breathe
Sit down in cypress shade
And breathe again

Then something smiles
Something, then, has changed

Conegliano Veneto, Italy, July 2019.[34]

---

34   Photo by the author.

Ibiza hills are not all that high, but they sure are as tough as any other, especially on a warm day...

Climbing Hot Old Hills

One more step is not too hard to make
Though heart thumps, chest heaves
And muscles burn and ache

These old volcanic hills are round -
Under the flail of August's sun
White rock glares, mirages abound

This sun beats harsh on head and back
And while the gradient slowly softens
The incline never flattens
But curves more gently up and on
One more skyline further
Beware the shorter path
The longer way is kinder

Don't be fooled, don't rush on
Another rise, another bend
Another, higher brow
And then
Another yet to follow

There is a place near the top where the going
        gets tougher
Harsher, steeper, rougher
Prone to sliding underfoot

And thick with jagged branch and root
Growing tired, looking up, distance seems
      now lengthened
And looking back down again, the giddy slope
      has steepened

Anxiety nags, grows, attacks
To meet the challenge, go on, go up
Or, reluctantly turn back?
You stop to breathe, you look about
Gaze to the flat horizon of the sea
Take stock to think it out

The things you see out there are two
That which you perceive to be
And that which lies apart from you

There is a place near the top where the going
      gets tougher
But cool is the air you breathed, and sweet
The ridge you saw so high before
Has dropped a little nearer
And from where you are you see a friend
Atop it, gazing out to sea

Santa Eulària des Riu, May-July 2019.

Immeasurably important things that maybe once you knew but are lost beyond memory to you in your present form...

Once the World Showed You Something

Once the world showed you a precious thing
But you have forgotten
It is there in your half remembered dreams
In moments of Déjà Vu
Unexplained recognition
Sudden longings
Something to which you can't put a name
Or a picture, or a face
One day, maybe, you will remember
And on that day
You will feel
A loss beyond conception

One day someone was there, and asking
If you needed anything
And you declined
Then she was no longer there
You closed your eyes, for centuries
And waited
But she never came
And now her face is lost in cloud
You think sometimes you catch
The scent of her skin on the air
And although you don't know who or what
You hope one day she will again be there

That is the day you will know
Joy beyond conception

Once the world showed you something
Remember, remember

Santa Eulària des Riu, Eivissa, August 2019.[35]

35 Artwork: *A Woman Holding a Wineglass in a Doorway* by Pieter de Hooch
(ca. 1675–1680), from Wikimedia Commons. Public domain.

Some are happy and at peace walking a comfortable, unchallenging path through life. Others need a harsher, wilder road to travel...

Traveller

The traveller
On the road
Is not sorry
It is not his nature to seek peace
By the fountains of caravanserais
For very long
He is young
Young enough
To hunger for the Golden Road; to face
Its harshness and its trials
Where any peace
Lies unknown
In another place
Beyond the dust his footsteps raise
Beyond those hills where the four winds cry

Santa Eulària des Riu, Eivissa, August 2019.

In August 2019 a 15-year-old girl with special needs tragically went missing from a forest resort in Malaysia. Her body was found lying near a waterfall in the jungle. I had visited the same resort on two different occasions and had become familiar with the area where she was found...

Sleeping by the Waterfall

Sleeping by the waterfall
Darling little one
The river singing for you softly
Its forever song

You had hardly lived
Before you had to go
But the world showed you secrets
Only made for you

Dreams floating by like jewels
Sweet shadowed memories
Do you see the flowers
In those mystery hills of green?

Remember the mist after rain?
The darting of the swifts?
And Gecko on the ceiling
Going chik-chik-chik-chik-chik?

Asleep by the waterfall
You precious little one
Butterflies dance above your brow
A journey just begun

Can you hear the call of the doo-doo-doo
     bird?
The insects whistling out of sight?
The laughter of the evening frogs
And the thousand sounds of night?

Sunlight patterns through the leaves
A leaf floats to your chest
Carried like you, our little one
On fragrant air of East

You had hardly lived at all
Before you had to go
But the world showed you secrets
Only made for you

You saw it all with priceless eyes
Left magic dust on Earth
Now carry your jewels with open hands

Across the universe

Sleeping by the waterfall
Darling little one
The river singing for you softly
Its forever song

Santa Eulària des Riu, Eivissa, August 2019.[36]

---

36 Image: Background photo of waterfall by the author. Superimposed photo of girl sleeping from Maxpixels.net, reproduced according to Creative Commons licence CC0 (https://creativecommons.org/publicdomain/zero/1.0/legalcode).

In the morning light, she lay beautifying the early sun's rays which played across her body...

Beckoning a Lover's Kiss

You lay eyes closed but not asleep
A quarter moon of darker skin peeps
Over the neckline of your cream negligee
Like a first edge of golden sun that slips
Above the pearly morning mist
Beckoning a lover's kiss

Rodney Stoke, England, August 2019.[37]

____

37 Photo by Philip Halling, *Misty sunrise over Worcester*, via Geograph.org.uk, reproduced according to Creative Commons licence CC BY-SA 2.0 (https:// creativecommons.org/licenses/by-sa/2.0/legalcode).

The Poplars Sing the Wind

A line of poplars sings the wind
Ssssssssshhhhhhhhhh
Flickering dark and pale
Leaves move, but the trees don't change
The gust moves the vale
A meadow, a willow, a field of maize
Rolling clouds, sunlight between
And the trees sing the wind
Ssssssssshhhhhhhhhh

August's end is drawing near
Alighted from their summer's flight
A line of swifts upon the wire
Turned to the wind-blown melody
Ssssssssshhhhhhhhhh

This wind's well-known by birds
But me, I can't make out the words
An ancient wall is in the way
It seems
There's something I can't reach at play
And the poplars sing the wind
Ssssssssshhhhhhhhhh

Rodney Stoke, England, August 2019.[38]

---

38 Photo by the author.

Experiencing the edge of consciousness...

Limbo

Reaching out
Neither in this place nor out
It's dark in between
They move but can't be seen

The play was well rehearsed
The players all well versed
But when the faded curtain folds
The wall against your hand is cold

A million far-off points of light
A million chances in a life
A million moons pass one by one
You move towards a rising sun

A whirlwind twists before your eyes
A rainbow shoots through purple skies
The choir's sweet song turns to noise
You climb out from the timeless void

Reaching back
Neither in this world nor that
Just a strange place in between
Where once you were the dream

Santa Eulària des Riu, Eivissa, September 2019.

When somebody realises they have been playing an active part in that so common kind of social interaction… ego-led and each indulging in our own little behavioural what-have-yous… and so decides to stop and just observe…

The Rehabilitation of Mr Jones

The hungry one-armed blacksmith's holy
    hammer strikes
Relentless, he's empty-eyed, his tongue is
    burning bright
The sparks fly wild and curling up into the
    night
His shadow slowly turns and heaves a tome

To the Bedouin queen, her white mare spins
    around
A spark is in her eye, her flaming hair is
    singed with brown
She yells 'Damn you, you thief', and spits on
    the ground
Then flies shrieking to the forest in the gloam

The jester wanders through, he's left behind
    by the court
He cries after the queen, "May I to the town
    be brought?"
He's looking for to charm, takes out his magic
    flute
Then runs in circles whistling to the moon

The satyagrahi's snoring, he wakes up with a
    start

Takes a slug of saintly wine and lets out a fart
He's garrulous tonight, wants to talk of love
      and art
Powerless to please, goes back to sleeping
      with a groan

The harpist's strings are broken, she will
      suffer not the din
From the clanging and snoring and the whistle
      made of tin
And the raging gypsy's curses have her ears
      buckling in
She lies down with the cat who's purring on
      the stone

A man walks in the room, he's put on weight
      and how
Takes his eyes out of his pocket, picks his face
      off the ground
You turn to see him better, but you are him
      now
He's smiling, amused you've come back all
      alone

Then you know something is happening and
      you know just what it is
Don't you Mr Jones?

Santa Eulària des Riu, Eivissa, September 2019.[39]

---

39 With apologies to Bob Dylan's *Ballad of a Thin Man* (1965).

To those mean and selfish people who enclose their properties so close to the cliff edge as to prevent passage on foot along the coastal way...

Must Have Wings

Must have wings
Herman wrote
On the parapet
He wants the abyss
My eye

House?
A fortress I say
De luxe of course
And extensive
My design
MINE

Protected
With botanical prickles
From the outersphere
Who goes there?
I will snare you too
With spikes and wire

Critical corridor done for
Shall not pass
The impersonal is far down
Heave you away
Unwinged annoyance

Santa Eulària des Riu, Eivissa, August 2019.[40] [41]

---

40 Man muss flügel haben, wenn man den abgrund liebt (Man must have wings
    if he loves the abyss). Friedrich Wilhelm Nietzsche.
41 Photo by the author.

While walking down by the river, I encountered a man in a wheelchair. His carer was sitting next to him on a bench. The look in the face of that man was terrible, pitifully begging to be relieved of his eternal agony, while knowing that any such hope was forlorn...

Much Worse Than Death

Terror distorts the face
Limbs jump and shake
Of what should be a man
A twisted mouth that cannot speak
His awful pain
Insanely shrieks and whines
Yet the eyes are not insane
Living death?
This is much worse
Trapped in body that doesn't work

Santa Eulària des Riu, Eivissa, September 2019.

We all have to say sorry sometimes...

Bruised

Fallen petal, so beautiful, but bruised
By a stone kicked carelessly along the path
Sorrowful, I whisper to the petal
Lovingly, so it might heal

Santa Eulària des Riu, Eivissa, October 2019.[42]

---

42 Photo from Pxhere.com, reproduced according to Creative Commons licence CC0 1.0 (https://creativecommons.org/publicdomain/zero/1.0/legalcode).

Of those lives lived...

What's Left?

Pictures on the shelf
and snapshots in the head,
but they're gone
nine months now and so, so what?

Hopes exchanged as courting jewels,
plans set out and toil for goals
great enough to pay for years
of sacrifice, and all the strife
of life
with little joys
and so, so what?

Days at work
with blood of heart and sweat of hand,
and days away,
with boating on the lake
or by the sea, sitting on the sand.
Saturday morning trips to town,
Sunday kitchen, making lunch,
Martini Dry with just a touch
of gin, for luck
to help the cook.
Pastimes passed and interests fed
tapestries sewn, work in the shed
And holidays taken here or there,
photos from this place or that,

can't really remember where,
and so, so what?

A walk along the street,
people to see,
exchange words, have conversations
about the day this or that happened,
hello, goodbye, take care, so long,
relations lost, friends to meet
but blood's the closest bond,
or not.
So what?

Morning news on the radio,
laugh at your favourite TV show,
wait up for the weather forecast,
the wind will blow
from east or west,
or not,
there may be snow, let's hope
it doesn't last,
lottery numbers didn't come up,
again.
Damn and blast!
Maybe next time.
So what?

Thoughts thought, views expressed,
opinions, deeply entrenched,
or changed
because of that or this.
Words of wisdom, words of tenderness,

a sharp look, a sweet caress,
routines of life,
get up and go to bed.
So what?

Certificates, advancements
professional achievements
and the like of such
of which one was or might be proud
but never really talked about
too much.
And every landmark passed
raise a glass.
And then, so what?

What's left?
All those papers
from the chest
of drawers
that writhed and blackened in the flames,
that once had words and names,
they're gone
burned to ash and smoke,
and so, so what?

What's left?
Some pictures on the shelf
and snapshots in my head
and little else,
So what?

Except

there is
myself.

Santa Eulària des Riu, Eivissa, October 2019.[43]

---

43 Photo by "_Alicja_", via Pixabay, reproduced according to the Pixabay licence (https://pixabay.com/service/terms/#license).

Laugh at the raving down-and-out if you will, but only by chance
are you not that person…

Tramp

Only the tramp
walking in and out of El Falucho
feels meaning as he spits
his crackled words to the ground
as quickly as they abandon him
for the next crazy thought:
Spray like salt arcs slowly over water on a day
      of bluster
but the colour of the ocean is unchanging.

Although, maybe not...
Maybe someone sitting here
at one of El Falucho's white plastic tables
knew another time, when he,
invisible and lacking the courage of voice,
nurtured too the silent rage
at the smugness of a world blithe with the
      wind in its sails -
and understands the voice from throat of
      Tramp;
seeping up through vortices of circumstance
now issued forth by vocal cords deformed
by randomness and loathing
of self and a world of casual contempt
sitting now at white plastic tables
on a day of bluster
with the wind in its sails.

Maybe he watches himself walking in and out
    of El Falucho,

tattered and grimed rag of Man,

before time worn and bared of thread,

brave, raving, raging, random, hopeless,

aimless walker through white chairs

and ever onwards over red paving slabs,

whose thoughts leap like sea spray onto rocks

while the colour of the ocean stays
      unchanging.

Santa Eulària des Riu, Eivissa, October 2019.[44]

44 Artwork: *Head of a Tramp* by László Mednyánszky (ca. 1896), from Wikimedia Commons. Public domain.

Based on a report by Christina Lamb, which appeared in the Sunday Times on 6th October 2019, about Qudrat Wasefi, 20, a music teacher who plays his trumpet on top of "TV Mountain" in Kabul...

The Trumpeter of Kabul

Louis Armstrong
sounds across the city where music was
      banned.
People turn their eyes through haze
to the hill where the trumpeter stands,
a silhouette against a yellow day.
They laugh but then they stay
and listen, as the trumpet player plays
and Louis Armstrong floats
above the city where people kill
with guns and bombs. At least today
they're still.

Down in the streets the children can hear it.
In their homes mothers and fathers can hear it.
In the bazaars and the teashops
the poor and the rich can hear it.
In the station and the barracks
the police and soldiers can hear it.
Out on the slopes
the Taliban and the warlords can hear it.
Gulbuddin Hekmatyar can hear it.
In the parliament buildings
the president can hear it.
The politicians can hear it.

The old and the young of the city can hear it,
especially the young,
who listen, in hope
to music, instead for once
of the noise of war.

Louis Armstrong
sounds across the city where music was
      banned.
People turn their eyes through haze
to the hill where the trumpeter stands,
a silhouette against a yellow day.
They laugh but then they stay.

Santa Eulària des Riu, Eivissa, October 2019.

A time of pain...

Dread the Night

The darkness used to be my friend
But now it comes with the mask of Seth
With its white hyena on a leash
To chew my flesh with its icy breath

Santa Eulària des Riu, Eivissa, November 2019.[45]

A time of illness...

Do Not Ask Me How I've Been

Do not ask me how I've been
But tell me instead
Of raging waves or singing streams
Of flowers, birdsong, towering clouds
Or sunbeams glanced through valley green
Then tell of yourself... Come on speak loud
Tell of your pain, your deepest need
Of how you are strong and how you are weak
Of your totems, taboos, affinities
What you hold dear and what do you fear
And as we share a full glass of wine
Maybe then you may hear of mine
Not how but who, not there but here
Then before you up and take your leave
We'll marvel together at great mysteries

Santa Eulària des Riu, Eivissa, November 2019.

For those starting out (once again?) on the great journey…

Ralph Lee

Ralph Lee
Born of the source
Thrust into the main stream

Now at the headwaters
Gentle, clear and sweet
Later the stream will widen
The flow strengthen
The depths sink to mystery and murk

You may climb up onto the bank
To move along a stretch on foot
You will need a big pair of boots
For you are all your fathers and mothers -
Along the river they have passed
Through time beyond imagination

So as you travel your path from source to
      estuary
One day to look out over the vast ocean
Remember this
And you will learn to fill those boots
And even need a larger size

May you honour your journey
And your journey honour you

Travel well
Ralph Lee

Santa Eulària des Riu, Eivissa, November 2019.[46]

---

46 Artwork by Margaret Hale (1929-2019), reproduced with permission of the estate of Margaret Hale.

About the Author

"While still on the road, learner, hunter of icicles, drinker of
Khayyam's wine, some kind of healer."

Robert grew up in the south of England before seeking his fortune
in foreign lands. His home now is on beautiful Ibiza with his
beloved Clouds Woman. He makes himself useful and earns a crust
by providing health care to the local community. He loves to spend
time walking the woods, cliffs and coastlines of his island home,
and torturing some apology for music out of his mandolin. He
loves solitude, bodies of water, forests, observing the beauty and
the harshness of nature, and (quixotically) pondering the
imponderable mysteries of life. His poetry is inspired by the beauty
and mystery of the world around us, the natural environment, the
human condition, and the greatest motivator of them all, love.
Robert has been published in several respected poetry magazines.
This is his third collection of poems. His previous collections, *No
Better Time Than This* and *The Storyteller of Isfahan* are also
published by Yabisa Gashouse. Robert's other works include a
guide to managing stress, a technical book on acupuncture, and an
online guide to the medicinal herbs of Ibiza (under perpetual
development).